What is Scientology?

History, Beliefs, Rules, Secrets and Facts

Boyd Grant

I want to dedicate this to my fiancée Sue. Thank you for the support you gave me while I put this book together.

Copyright © 2014 by Speedy Publishing LLC

All rights reserved. No part of this publication may be reproduced, distributed or transmitted in any form or by any means, including photocopying, recording, or other electronic or mechanical methods, without the prior written permission of the publisher, except in the case of brief quotations embodied in critical reviews and certain other noncommercial uses permitted by copyright law. For permission requests, write to the publisher, addressed "Attention: Permissions Coordinator," at the address below.

Speedy Publishing LLC (c) 2014
40 E. Main St., #1156
Newark, DE 19711
www.speedypublishing.co

Ordering Information:
Quantity sales; Special discounts are available on quantity purchases by corporations, associations, and others. For details, contact the "Special Sales Department" at the address above.

-- 1st edition

Manufactured in the United States of America

TABLE OF CONTENTS

PUBLISHER'S NOTES i

CHAPTER 1: INTRODUCTION 1

CHAPTER 2: HISTORY 3

CHAPTER 3: FUNDAMENTAL BELIEFS 8

CHAPTER 4: SYMBOLS 16

CHAPTER 5: AUDITING AND TRAINING EXPLAINED 18

CHAPTER 6: SUNDAY SERVICE 20

CHAPTER 7: WHY DO PEOPLE HATE THIS RELIGION? 23

CHAPTER 8: SCIENTOLOGY AND CONTROVERSY 26

CHAPTER 9: FORMER SCIENTOLOGY MEMBERS WILL NOT RECOMMEND THIS RELIGION 30

CHAPTER 10: THE SCIENTOLOGY FREE ZONE MOVEMENT 33

CHAPTER 11: WHY DO PEOPLE JOIN THE CHURCH OF SCIENTOLOGY? 35

CHAPTER 12: IS SCIENTOLOGY RIGHT FOR YOU? 37

MEET THE AUTHOR 38

Publisher's Notes

Disclaimer

This publication is intended to provide helpful and informative material. It is not intended to diagnose, treat, cure, or prevent any health problem or condition, nor is intended to replace the advice of a physician. No action should be taken solely on the contents of this book. Always consult your physician or qualified health-care professional on any matters regarding your health and before adopting any suggestions in this book or drawing inferences from it.

The author and publisher specifically disclaim all responsibility for any liability, loss or risk, personal or otherwise, which is incurred as a consequence, directly or indirectly, from the use or application of any contents of this book.

Any and all product names referenced within this book are the trademarks of their respective owners. None of these owners have sponsored, authorized, endorsed, or approved this book.

Always read all information provided by the manufacturers' product labels before using their products. The author and publisher are not responsible for claims made by manufacturers.

Print Edition 2014

Chapter 1: Introduction

There are a large number of misconceptions surrounding Scientology as a result of conspiracy theories and consistent media misrepresentation. Scientology is a means of achieving independence from attachment to anything in the material world, in order to reach a greater, higher substantial presence.

Scientology emphasizes self-knowledge as a means of realizing full spiritual potential. The word comes from **scient** (knowing; skillful) and "logy" "the study of." Scientology adheres to a "fundamental truth" which is that people have the ability to access completely new states of awareness outside of what they usually encounter.

Scientology believes that people, as spiritual beings, are capable of ascending beyond this world to attain spiritual freedom.

Scientology focuses on the fundamentals of mankind's existence, utilizing methodologies and beliefs that are common to the majority of the surviving religions worldwide. In Scientology, people are believed to be essentially good.

Scientology is a young religion-it was founded in the 20th century. Even though the religion was born in 1953, its followers believe it has roots in some of the oldest religions known throughout the world.

WHAT IS SCIENTOLOGY?

Scientology allows practitioners the opportunity to benefit from the knowledge of old religions and the efficiency of present day technologies. It combines the information gathered from the history of human communities and ancient civilizations, along with Eastern and Western philosophies, and incorporates it into new modern advances that can inspire mankind toward contentment, achievement and ultimately a higher spiritual existence.

CHAPTER 2: HISTORY

Scientology was founded by science fiction writer L. Ron Hubbard. As a young man Hubbard was a practitioner of ritual magic, the occult and hypnosis. According to his biography, at the age of 19 his thirst for knowledge led him to travel to Tibet, India and various Asian countries over the span of two years (1927-1929). Hubbard claims that he was deeply influenced by the holy men of those countries. He was introduced to the religious teachings of the Dalai Lama, Buddhist monks, and Hindu pundits (learned men) and priests. A meeting with a Chinese magician who was the last in the line of royal magicians connected to Kublai Khan further oriented him toward these spiritual practices.

Hubbard returned to the United States with what he'd learned from the teachings of the major Eastern religions. Hubbard concluded that mankind, amidst the immense wisdom it has gathered throughout the ages, had reached a degraded state, and that deprivation is the result of the congruence between the mind and the body. Man is a spirit, he said, an entity that can fulfill his true potential through the realization that some aspects of life exist beyond the physical realm.

Hubbard combined personal experience, the fundamentals of Eastern philosophy, and the work of Freud and other psychoanalysts to create Dianetics. Hubbard coined the term Dianetics from the Greek stems *dia*, and *nous*, meaning – "through soul." Dianetics is a combination of Western technology and Oriental philosophy.

The theory behind Dianetics is that memories, called *engrams* are stored in our "reactive" mind and need to be moved to our "analytical" mind. This can be done through a process called *auditing*, where a "patient" and an "auditor" undergo two-way interview sessions. Auditing is a form of psychotherapy that allows an individual to relive past traumatic experiences, come to terms with them, and release them. Auditing paves the way for the patient to unleash his potential and achieve spiritual enlightenment.

In 1949, Hubbard's work on Dianetics was published in the Winter/Spring issue of *The Explorers Club Journal*. Hubbard offered his findings to the American Medical Association and the American Psychiatric Association, but they were rejected by both organizations. In 1950, Hubbard published *Dianetics: The Modern Science of Mental Health* which became a worldwide best seller.

The Dianetics movement quickly found momentum, and in June 1951 the Hubbard Dianetics Research Foundation was established in Elizabeth, New Jersey. Dianetics centers were established in various areas of the United States, and many people became staunch followers of the movement in an attempt to enrich their lives. The scientific and medical communities did not support Hubbard's work.

In 1952, Hubbard was forced to shut down his foundation due to disagreements among board members, and legal problems. Constant criticism from the medical community resulted in the New Jersey Board of Medical Examiners filing a legal suit against Hubbard's organization for teaching medicine without a license. The board of directors voted to file for voluntary bankruptcy, over Hubbard's objections. The declaration of bankruptcy resulted in Hubbard no longer owning the rights to the name Dianetics.

Within the same year, Hubbard relocated to Phoenix, Arizona. He demonstrated the E-meter (a kind of lie detector used by auditors to examine a person's mental state) and published a new set of teachings called *Scientology: A History of Man*.

Dianetics would not be replaced by Scientology; it quickly evolved into an extension of Scientology, covering new and different areas. Hubbard claimed to have discovered methods to free the soul from its entrapment in the physical or material world and allow man to unleash his full potential as a spirit separate from the body. Scientology applies the methods of Dianetics.

Dianetics was still rejected by the medical community, but in 1954 the Church of Scientology was accepted as a religion and was established in Los Angeles, California. In 1956, Scientology was officially declared a religion and was granted US federal tax-exempt status. This was a major victory for Hubbard. The IRS began investigating the Church of Scientology in 1958. In 1959, Hubbard purchased Saint Hill Mansion in Sussex, England. From Sussex, he oversaw international operations and expansion.

In 1960, the Hubbard Mark II E-Meter was released. It was soon followed by the Hubbard Mark III E-Meter. Three years later, the US Food and Drug Administration raided the Original Founding Church of Scientology and all of the Church's E-meters, when it was discovered that they were being used as medical devices illegally.

Hubbard also ran into trouble after founding Narconon, a drug rehab center.

In 1967, The Sea Organization (or Sea Org) was officially established. The Sea Org was Hubbard's inner circle-an elite group within the Church of Scientology (a particularly zealous branch of Scientology, which is too complex and controversial to cover here).

In the same year, the IRS stripped Scientology of its tax-exempt status, claiming that its related activities were operated for Hubbard's financial gain rather than for religious or charitable causes.

In 1969, the U.S. Court of Appeals turned everything upside down. The FDA lost Scientology vs. the FDA, and Scientology was declared a religion.

The Church of Scientology Celebrity Center in Los Angeles, California was founded in 1970. In 1971, the FDA was ordered by the courts to return the materials and E-meters seized during the 1963 raid. The E-meters are now required to carry a disclaimer saying that they are religious artifacts and are not intended for medical use.

Scientology was in the news again in 1984 after some members quit the church and publicly accused Hubbard of lying about his life and diverting money to foreign bank accounts.

Hubbard passed away in 1986 after suffering a stroke at his ranch near San Luis Obispo, California. David Miscavige quickly took over as chairman of the board of the Religious Technology Center, effectively assuming control of the church.

In 1993 the IRS settled its 40-year battle with Scientology and recognized its churches as tax-exempt.

Scientology Is Currently Recognized As A Religion In The Following Countries:

- Australia
- Croatia
- Hungary
- Kyrgyzstan
- Portugal
- Republic of China (Taiwan)
- Slovenia
- Spain
- Sweden
- United States of America

The Church of Scientology is thought of as a religious cult by some. Due to the somewhat secretive nature of the church, Scientologists' beliefs are often unknown or misunderstood by the general public.

CHAPTER 3: FUNDAMENTAL BELIEFS

Scientology's Version of Creation

Scientology, like most religions, has its version of how humans, life and the universe were created. According to Scientology, today's world is reflective of the four components of creation: matter, energy, space and time.

The doctrine of Scientology makes a passing reference to a Supreme Being (who is also referred to as Infinity) and it represents the universal survival instinct. Scientology is based on its own mythology and teaches that people are immortal beings who have forgotten their true nature. Scientology revolves around the concept of a thetan, or spirit, and less emphasis is placed upon the Supreme Being. Thetans, or the life force, "created the material world for satisfaction of their own pleasure in a primordial past."

Basically, Scientology is about thetans (human souls) regaining their spiritual power.

View on the Spirit, the Mind and the Body

Scientology's central belief is, "humans are intrinsically good, non-material, all knowing and are armed with limitless creativity."

The term thetans was derived from theta-theta is a Greek letter that represents the life or cosmic source.

Like Hindus and Buddhists, Scientologists believe that the physical body is nothing more than a temporary body for the thetan. They believe in a process called "assumption," which is comparable to reincarnation. They also emphasize the belief in the effects of past and present actions that affect future life, which closely resembles karma.

Throughout the different lifetimes of a thetan, several images (or engrams) are stored in that spiritual being's memory. They are generally painful and destructive to the thetan. They are also instrumental in keeping the thetan further away from his or her true identity.

The basic goal of the thetan is to restore its true identity. Thetans accomplish this by undertaking personal spiritual development.

Spiritual development has two phases: training and processing. Training is the introduction to the principles of auditing, which provides the path to a higher state of spiritual awareness. Members practice the principles of auditing in the processing phase.

Scientologists refer to these two phases of spiritual development as The Bridge to Total Freedom. It requires and enables the attainment of high moral and ethical standards.

Scientology's concept of the mind comes from the Freudian concept of the subconscious. To Scientologists, this is called the "reactive mind," which naturally responds to painful experiences in an irrational and emotional manner.

The concept of God in Scientology is different from the concepts observed by religions such as Christianity and Islam. Scientology teaches that each member, as a thetan, can and will become a god with sufficient spiritual enlightenment and growth.

Morals and Ethics

Scientology places high value on actions that encourage well-being among the largest number of individuals while reducing suffering. Scientologists believe in striving for the "greater good" of mankind and the universe. Unlike most other religions, rationality is ranked above emotion and morality. In Scientology, morals are a collectively agreed-upon code of good conduct; ethics are defined as "the actions an individual takes in order to accomplish optimum survival according to the Dynamics, which first benefits the self and eventually, ultimately benefits all living things, the planet, and the universe as a whole."

1st Dynamic: Self

Individual survival instinct.

2nd Dynamic: Creativity

Reproduction, sex and the family unit.

3rd Dynamic: Group Survival

The creation and survival of super organisms (communities, friends, nations, races, etc.).

4th Dynamic: Species

The survival of mankind.

5th Dynamic: Life Forms

The survival of all living things including plants, animals, birds, insects, etc.

6th Dynamic: Physical Universe

The survival of the physical universe itself.

7th Dynamic: Spiritual Universe

The survival of the spiritual self, spiritual beings and the spiritual universe.

8th Dynamic: Infinity

The Supreme Being/Creator.

In accordance with the 8 Dynamics, sacrificing yourself and/or your friends and family in order to save the lives of others would be a logical decision as a part of Scientology's belief in rationality above emotion.

Scientologists aspire to dedicate themselves to the well-being of others over their own personal interests. Adhering to this doctrine at all times is known to be virtually impossible. Therefore, the 8 Dynamics are seen as an ideal that Scientologists should strive to live by rather than as a rigorous code of conduct.

Achievement Levels

Scientology focuses more on practical application in one's life against worship or codes of conduct. This practical application involves spiritual evolution and advancement.

Scientology is divided into the following achievement levels:

- Preclear
- Clear
- Operating Thetan

Preclear

The level that all members start out in is Preclear. Members go through auditing sessions to eliminate engrams.

Clear

Reaching level Clear requires a lot of time, many auditing sessions and additional Dianetic requirements.

According to Scientology doctrine, level Clear allows an individual to exist in a higher state of spiritual and mental capability. Hubbard describes Clear status as "a being that no longer has his own reactive mind, and therefore suffers none of the ill effects the reactive mind can cause."

Reaching level Clear comes with a cost, estimated between $125,000 and $130,000 U.S. dollars. All fees or payments to the church are "donations."

Operating Thetan

Operating Thetan, also referred to as OT, consists of many sub levels that allow people to continue their spiritual journey. The known levels of Operating Thetan are OT I through OT VIII. There are allegedly seven additional levels, up to OT XV.

The goal of Operating Thetan status is referred to as Cleared Theta Clear. This spiritual and mental state is described as, "A thetan that is completely rehabilitated and can do everything a thetan should do, such as move MEST (matter, energy, space, time) and control others from a distance, or create his own universe."

Anyone who reaches the level of Cleared Theta Clear will become like the original thetans and will no longer be bound by the physical universe, making him or her a god-like being.

It should be noted that - there have been no reports of anyone ever reaching this state.

Mental States

In the doctrine of Scientology, there are two principal mental states:

Reactive Mind

Analytical Mind

The reactive mind is the portion of the mind that stores painful emotional memories (engrams) and acts upon these memories. These actions usually result in negative consequences.

The analytical mind is the portion of the mind that functions rationally (and preferably in accordance with the 8 Dynamics).

Members of the Church of Scientology are encouraged to embrace the rational mind while dealing with the reactive mind by other means, such as auditing and other practices using Dianetics.

Personalities

The Church of Scientology has an interesting view on human nature. According to the doctrine, roughly 80 percent of humanity has "social personalities" which contribute to the greater good and welfare of others. The other 20 percent of humanity are "suppressive personalities" and actively harm others. According to Hubbard, only about 2.5 percent of that 20 percent are irredeemable individuals (such as true sociopaths and psychopaths).

Scientology's doctrine dictates that contact with a suppressive personality at any level is harmful to one's spiritual condition. Therefore contact with suppressive personalities is discouraged.

It should be pointed out that there are no objective standards in the doctrine describing what constitutes a social personality and what constitutes a suppressive personality, which leaves room for interpretation, though members who defect from the Church of Scientology and become outspoken critics of it are often labeled as suppressive personalities. Additionally, church members who maintain contact with someone deemed a suppressive personality may be labeled as a "potential trouble source."

Scientology vs. Psychology

Scientology is strongly opposed to psychology and psychiatry, and has been since its inception.

The Church of Scientology considers psychiatric care abusive and counterproductive to natural spiritual healing. Scientology's criticism of these medical fields has generated a great deal of controversy over the years.

Throughout the years, Scientology's war on psychology has included failed attempts to infiltrate the National Association of Mental Health in Britain, the World Federation for Mental Health, and the National Association of Mental Health in a drive to turn national policy against all forms of mental health treatment.

Scientologists are required to sign documents and legal waivers that forbid them to seek any form of psychiatric or psychological treatment. Below is an excerpt from a waiver obtained as part of a 2003 media report on that topic:

"I do not believe in or subscribe to psychiatric labels for individuals. It is my strongly held religious belief that all mental problems are spiritual in nature and that there is no such thing as a mentally incompetent person—only those suffering from spiritual upset of one kind or another dramatized by an individual.

I reject all psychiatric labels and intend for this contract to clearly memorialize my desire to be helped exclusively through religious, spiritual means and not through any form of psychiatric treatment, specifically including involuntary commitment based on so-called lack of competence. Under no circumstances, at any time, do I wish to be denied my right to care from members of my religion to the exclusion of psychiatric-care or psychiatric directed care, regardless of what any psychiatrist, medical person, designated member of the state or family member may assert supposedly on my behalf."

Religious Ceremonies and Holidays

Official religious ceremonies are optional in Scientology. Official ceremonies are less common than other religions, and they play a relatively small part in the religious lives of Scientologists.

In addition to religious services, the Church of Scientology also performs weddings, funerals, and child naming. These services are performed by the church's ordained ministers.

Scientologists celebrate Hubbard's birthday in March, the anniversary of the first publication of *Dianetics* in May, and Auditor's Day in September. Scientologists are welcome to celebrate the religious holidays that they were raised with, as well as secular holidays and local celebrations.

CHAPTER 4: SYMBOLS

Scientology's main symbol is a cross and star with four spikes, which together form an eight-pointed star representing the 8 Dynamics. The eight-pointed star is also a representation of Chaos both in fiction and in some esoteric religions.

ARC and KRC Triangles

The ARC and KRC triangles are concept maps that show a relationship among three concepts to form another concept. The two triangles are intertwined in the Scientology "S" as seen in the symbol below.

ARC is a basic term in Scientology, and a concept and symbol that every Scientologist understands. The letters ARC are a representation of the knowledge Scientologists strive for. It encompasses Affinity (affection, love or liking), Reality (consensual reality) and Communication (the exchange of ideas). Scientologists believe that improving one of the three aspects of the triangle increases the level of the other two, but Communication is held to be the most important.

Scientology believes that social problems are due to breakdowns in ARC. A lack of agreement on reality, a failure to communicate effectively, or a failure to develop affinity can produce harmful acts against another, either intentionally or by omission, which are usually followed by withholds or efforts to conceal the wrongdoing, which further increase the level of tension in a relationship.

ARC is sometimes used as a term of affection in communications by Scientologists; it may be found, at the end of an email.

The points in the KRC triangle are K for Knowledge, R for Responsibility and C for Control. According to this concept, it is difficult to be Responsible for something or Control something unless you have Knowledge of it. It is foolish to try to Control something or even Know something without Responsibility. It is hard to Know something or be Responsible for something over which you have no Control. Scientology teaches that by increasing Knowledge, Responsibility and Control in all dynamics, over time, one can make anything go right.

Hubbard referred to the ARC and KRC triangles as "magic triangles." Alter one corner of the triangle to cause a change in the other two corners. The alteration in the triangles can produce a "positive" or a "negative" effect.

Chapter 5: Auditing and Training Explained

Scientology is no different from other religions in its belief in the salvation of the spiritual being. However, the principles that govern Scientology's concept of salvation are distinct from those practiced by other religions. The central process of Scientology believes in training routes and methodologies that help individuals achieve Total Freedom.

Auditing

Auditing is considered the ultimate route for achieving higher states of spiritual awareness in Scientology. The goal in this process is to rehabilitate the physical being and allow the thetan or pure spirit to manifest. This will restore the innate qualities of the thetan, which are unlimited, like goodness, and omniscience. Without auditing, Scientologists believe these qualities cannot be brought back to their original states.

Auditing works by deleting the painful experiences of a Scientologist. In Scientology, a person is believed to have three different minds: the reactive mind, the analytical mind, and the somatic mind. The analytical mind is the component that observes, analyzes, and is generally responsible for thinking. The reactive mind is, if translated from a Freudian perspective, the subconscious mind. The subconscious collects traumatic and painful experiences that hamper a person from becoming spiritually aware. This buildup is also what causes illnesses and psychosomatic disorders to manifest in the body. The solution is to delete this collection of traumatic experience through the methodologies prescribed by auditing.

An auditor is either a minister or a minister in training in any of Scientology's churches. The auditor listens to the individual as he clears his or her reactive mind and gives auditing commands.

The auditing technique uses tools called *processes,* which are a set of questions or directions given by an auditor to help the subject address the specific problems that are causing them spiritual distress. These questions are directed toward resolving any questions the subject may have regarding-the self, life, and the universe.

The process of auditing ends when the specific objective of the current process has been achieved. Another process may then be called for to address other issues or barriers that are inhibiting a person from becoming "clear" (which is essentially a state similar to enlightenment).

During the entire process of auditing, the subject remains conscious and alert. Auditors follow a strict code of conduct called the Auditor's Code, which is said to ensure the success of each session.

Training

A complimentary process to auditing is training. Auditing lets the subject see why some things happen; training teaches why they happen. Training is the stage where the knowledge gained while learning about Scientology is applied. By becoming trained, a Scientologist can better see the truths upheld by the religion.

CHAPTER 6: SUNDAY SERVICE

Church of Scientology of London

Like other religions, Scientology has a designated day for congregation. This is called the Sunday service. The Church of Scientology welcomes people of all religions and beliefs to their Sunday service.

The Sunday service is viewed as a focal point for uniting all the members of the religion on a single day. This is the day when they participate in their local churches to hear messages of inspiration, teachings, and to pray as one.

The Sunday service consists of many different parts. It is officiated by a chaplain or a minister once a week. The church's leader will speak about a topic related to the beliefs of the religion and explain how the lesson can be applied to day-to-day living. The intent of the service is to inspire members. Similar to the Catholic's Sunday Mass, Scientology's Sunday services include readings and a sermon.

The Recitation of the Creed of the Church of Scientology

Scientology follows a specific creed. The recitation or reading of this creed, from the writings of L. Ron Hubbard, starts every Sunday service. The creed affirms the aims of Scientology as a religion, outlines the missions of the church, allows members to rededicate themselves to the church, and outlines the expectations from members of the church.

The Sermon

Hubbard delivered at least 3,000 lectures that detail his path to the founding of Scientology. These teachings are used by the chaplain or minister as the basis for the sermon and are reworked so that they are current and relevant to the present conditions of society and each individual. The goal of the sermon is to inspire members and non-members to achieve a higher level of spiritual awareness and an increased understanding of how to apply the church's teachings in everyday life. An alternative to live sermons is playing recorded lectures, which were made by Hubbard years ago.

Group Auditing

Group auditing is part of the typical Sunday Service. The chaplain or minister conducting the service as the group auditor. The auditor gives a set of commands aimed at increasing the awareness of the participants so they can rid themselves of material possessions and become more spiritual.

Announcements

The Church of Scientology conducts activities outside of the religion itself. These activities often include community outreach events. The chaplain or minister will announce the schedule of activities during the Sunday service to remind members of their individual obligations to the church and to their communities.

Prayer

The prayer concludes the Sunday service. All Sunday services include The Prayer for Total Freedom. This prayer expresses what Scientology can achieve for its followers and is led by the chaplain or minister.

CHAPTER 7: WHY DO PEOPLE HATE THIS RELIGION?

Strong feeling towards a particular religion (especially strong negative feelings) are nothing new. Some people simply have no interest in organized religion-period! The hate directed towards Scientology bears no resemblance to the misunderstanding and judgment people aim at other major religions. Why do people hate Scientology so much?

Most people are only aware of Scientology because of celebrities who openly declare their affiliation with the controversial religion: Tom Cruise, Kirstie Alley, John Travolta, Will Smith, Lisa Maria Presley, and Nicolas Cage, to name a few. The Church of Scientology has subjected itself to criticisms from the media by targeting celebrities to increase their influence on society.

Hubbard envisioned early on that celebrities would play a key role in the dissemination of Scientology. In 1955, Hubbard launched Project Celebrity. A list of 63 famous people was created; they were targeted for conversion to Scientology. Former silent screen star Gloria Swanson and jazz pianist Dave Brubeck were among the earliest celebrities attracted to Hubbard's teachings. Using celebrities to introduce and educate the general public has been successful, but it is a tactic that some feel reeks of desperation.

Scientology currently operates eight churches that are designated Celebrity Centers. The largest is located in Hollywood. Celebrity Centers are open to the general public, but are primarily designed to attract and cater to celebrity Scientologists. Many people have speculated that celebrities join for tax-evasion purposes.

Critics of Scientology believe Hubbard founded the organization on lies, and that Dianetics is nothing more than psychiatry renamed and modified. As a result, Scientology is widely referred to as a scam and a cult.

The "scam" designation may be unfair. A scam is defined as a ploy by an opportunistic individual or group that aims to take advantage of people through trickery. Scientology does not conceal its basic core beliefs and principals or the requirement of auditing sessions. The price of the auditing sessions is not hidden, and is often listed within promotional materials. A member can pay for auditing on a per session basis and can stop at any time if they do not have the finances to proceed. Scientology collects donations from its members under the premise of improving the conditions of the church. All major religions do the same.

Former members of Scientology claim that it is necessary to give large sums of money in exchange for more advanced Scientology literature. For a Scientologist to achieve complete "enlightenment," specific books are needed for advancement and the church limits the availability of these materials. Current Scientologists deny these allegations and claim that money given to the church in exchange for items is a "donation." This is where the terms "scam" and "cult" begin to hold some credibility. As members are slowly drawn deeper into the church, over time, more and more money is required to reach the next level of spirituality.

Some claim that the Church of Scientology gives preferential treatment to celebrities and members with generous fortunes.

Is the Church of Scientology is a religion? Or a business? The church considers itself a religious institution, but many believe Scientology is merely a well-run, deceptively organized cult that hides behind religion for the sole purpose of making money.

CHAPTER 8: SCIENTOLOGY AND CONTROVERSY

Since the Church of Scientology's modest beginnings, Scientologists have been mixed up in scandals, allegations, crimes, and controversy.

This chapter will take a look at some of the elements that plague The Church of Scientology.

L. Ron Hubbard

The sincerity and honesty of the religion's founder is questioned by many. It is now well documented that the official biography of his life as told by the Church of Scientology contains factual errors about his university education, academic credentials, his naval service and other details. Some view Scientology as part therapy, part religion, part UFO group, while others question whether Scientology is nothing more than a product of Hubbard's skill as a science fiction writer, self-promoter and entrepreneur.

Xenu

This Scientology doctrine has been a constant source of contention. The doctrine was considered highly confidential material. It was leaked by former members in 1972 (and again in 1993).

In short, the doctrine teaches that 75 million years ago, the cosmic ruler Xenu paralyzed billions of people in our galaxy, stacked them on Earth and destroyed their physical bodies with hydrogen bombs. The disembodied thetan souls were captured and brainwashed with concepts such as God, the Devil and other religious material. (This "misleading data" as Hubbard called it, became known as the R6 implant.) The brainwashing caused thetans to lose their sense of individuality and become corrupted.

Referred to in the Scientology doctrine as Incident II or "The Wall of Fire," this story is only taught to those who have completed various requirements and have advanced to a higher level. The doctrine was previously available only to high-ranking members who paid thousands of dollars to the Church, but thanks to the Internet, it is now widely known.

Since the leak of the Xenu story the church has not discussed its existence-except to claim copyright of the story as confidential religious material. Some Scientologists, claim that the story is not meant to be taken literally, and it is a metaphor meant to help with spiritual progression.

Operation Snow White

Operation Snow White was a systematic attempt to infiltrate and steal classified files on Scientology from governments all over the world. Hubbard wanted unfavorable records about himself and Scientology members purged. The operation was carried out by church members in more than 30 countries during a brief period in the 70's. Multiple federal crimes were committed: infiltration, wiretapping and theft of documents in government offices.

Eleven high-ranked Church of Scientology executives pleaded guilty or were convicted in federal court of obstructing justice, burglary of government offices, and theft of documents and government property. Amongst the eleven convicted was the second-in-command-in the operation, Mary Sue Hubbard, wife of founder L. Ron Hubbard.

Secrecy

Per church policy, members of this religion do not speak about Scientology other than to offer direct quotes from Hubbard. The secrecy requirement tends to arouse suspicion.

The Cost of Scientology

The auditing process initially costs hundreds of dollars and progresses into the thousands as one moves "up the bridge" to the highest levels of awareness and teaching. Critics see this as a mechanism for brainwashing and acquiring quick wealth more than a means of helping people achieve spiritual freedom.

Attack the Attacker

The Church of Scientology has a reputation for hostile action toward anyone who criticizes it in a public forum. Attack the Attacker is a policy instituted by Hubbard in the 1960's in response to government investigations into the organization. Journalists, politicians, and former Scientologists who have made accusations of wrongdoings against Scientology have received responses in the form of lawsuits and public counter accusations of personal wrong doing. Many former members who've gone public claim they were subjected to private threats and harassment.

Consider one use of the policy on a broad scale-the Anderson Report was an inquiry conducted in 1965 for the State of Victoria, Australia, written by Kevin Victor Anderson QC. It concluded that "Scientology is a delusional belief system, based on fiction and fallacies and propagated by falsehood and deception" and that it "is not, and does not claim to be, a religion."

In response, the Church of Scientology published *Kangaroo Court*, which alleged collusion between witnesses and bias by Anderson. The Hubbard Association of Scientologists filed a lawsuit against Kevin Anderson and his assistant, Gordon Just.

Authority Within the Church

The Church safeguards the copyrights and intellectual property of Hubbard's ideas and strictly controls not only access to them, but also their interpretation and application in the religious life of adherents. It actively seeks out legal prosecution against those it believes are spreading their teachings and/or practices without permission.

When mainstream media has reported alleged abuses of church members, the church tends to respond by claiming an alleged agenda with the goal to misrepresent the organization's intentions.

Chapter 9: Former Scientology Members Will Not Recommend This Religion

Below are a few of the most common (alleged) reasons why former Scientologists will not recommend this religion:

Scientology asserts that it gives its members the freedom to make their own decisions in regard to their beliefs. Former members claim that once a person becomes a member, these freedoms are non-existent.

Once you are in, it is very difficult to get out. Former members claim that if or when you try to leave the religion, you may receive threats, you may be framed for criminal acts you did not commit, you and your family may be harassed, and your civil rights may be violated. This is the organization's "Fair Game" policy. It is an attempt to silence anyone who gives the Church of Scientology bad publicity or chooses to leave.

In one of the religion's scriptural texts, the "Introduction to Scientology Ethics," any criticism, anti-Scientology texts, letters, speeches, and testifying publicly against the religious cult are categorized as "Suppressive Acts." These are high crimes and are punishable according to the laws of the religion.

Scientology has a disconnection policy that orders its members to stop all communications with one's family members or friends if any of them are antagonistic against the religion or express anything negative against Scientology.

Scientology is not about religion. It is about making money. According to former members, the religion will drain you until you have sold your house, your car and maybe even yourself. Scientology will strip you of all of your possessions because one of the core beliefs of the religion tells its members that they must rid themselves of all materialistic possessions in order to be able to reach a higher spiritual state.

Los Angeles Superior Court Judge Paul G. Breckenridge ruled in October 1984 that Scientology is a religious cult and "a vast enterprise to extract maximum amount of money" from its members. Judge Breckenridge went on to say the following about L. Ron Hubbard:

"The evidence portrays a man who has been virtually a pathological liar when it comes to his history, background and achievements. The writings and documents in evidence additionally reflect his egoism, greed, avarice, lust for power, and vindictiveness and aggressiveness against persons perceived by him to be disloyal or hostile. At the same time it appears that he is charismatic and

highly capable of motivating, organizing, controlling, manipulating and inspiring his adherents. He has been referred to during the trial as a "genius," a "revered person," a man who was viewed by his followers in awe. Obviously, he is and has been a very complex person and that complexity is further reflected in his alter ego, the Church of Scientology."

L. Ron Hubbard, Jr., son of the religion's founder, claims the above is true, along with many other members who have seen and experienced Scientology from the inside.

Members who have left or been dismissed from any organization or club often tend to have negative or jaded views about former associates or practices of that organization. Keep this in mind when researching the Church of Scientology.

CHAPTER 10: THE SCIENTOLOGY FREE ZONE MOVEMENT

If you can identify with the concepts of Scientology but are uneasy about the controversy surrounding the organization, you may want to look into the Scientology Free Zone. The Scientology Free Zone is a movement that focuses on the original concepts that L. Ron Hubbard developed in his search for enlightenment.

The Scientology Free Zone was formed by former members who left the church by choice, those who were dismissed by the church, and others with a healthy amount of skepticism.

The Free Zone Movement encourages members to pursue enlightenment and personal growth based on the original philosophies developed by Hubbard, but without the authoritative and rigid system and principals of the church. Free Zone members believe that many of the theories Hubbard developed have been changed to fit the needs of a "corrupt" organization. Movement members feel that over the course of time, the true meaning of the church has become lost.

The Free Zone Movement was established in the early 1980s. The primary instigator of the movement was Captain Bill Robertson, a former Sea Org member. The Free Zone Movement claims to have a consistent increase in memberships, while numbers for the Church of Scientology decrease.

The Church of Scientology believes that unauthorized distribution of information about their practices will endanger mankind. Breakaway groups that practice Scientology outside of the official Church without authorization are labeled as "squirrels," in Scientology jargon. Breakaway groups are subjected to legal and social pressures by the Church.

The Free Zone Movement may be a source of frustration for the church, but it lacks support and funding. The Church of Scientology has name recognition, resources, and celebrity star power, making it is doubtful that the Free Zone Movement will ever overtake the church in popularity or members.

Chapter 11: Why Do People Join The Church Of Scientology?

There are many reasons why people align with any organized religion. Scientology has its own level of attraction.

Scientology offers its members ideas, beliefs, and principles that speak to certain individuals. The recruitment process promotes and highlights the benefits of the church to prospective members. The idea of attaining a godlike state is very attractive to some; while others may be seek to achieve a higher spiritual awareness.

One of the marketing strategies the church deploys is offering members "solutions." Before any individual can join The Church of Scientology, they must take the Oxford Capacity Test, which is a personality test that assesses problems within the individual. The church will bait the recruit with solutions but help is only accessible if the individual becomes a member.

The controversy that surrounds the Church of Scientology actually draws certain individuals in. These members do not fit into traditional religions, organizations, or their family's "traditional" beliefs or values. They are impressed with the chance to be recruited, and they are reeled in by the organization's attractive facade and its members.

Some people are born into Scientology. These individuals are raised as Scientologists and it is the only religion that they have ever known. Scientologists are not allowed to explore principals or beliefs of other religions making individuals born into Scientology ignorant of other religions and possible options. Once they become aware of other possibilities, they may decide to leave, and leaving the church requires great effort and courage.

Chapter 12: Is Scientology Right for You?

The Church of Scientology claims to have a total of eight million followers worldwide. Controversy surrounds and follows this young religion but people are still attracted to its beliefs and principles. Most individuals have the freedom to choose and practice any religion they desire and one of the many options is Scientology.

Every religion has individuals and misunderstood concepts that reflect poorly on the religion and what it stands for, and Scientology is no exception.

The information in this book should be used for informational purposes only. It is not an attempt to sway readers to join Scientology, nor is it meant to convince people to steer clear of the organization.

Choosing a religion is a personal decision that is often based on perception, goals, life experiences, lifestyles, needs and expectations.

When someone has gathered enough research and information to make an informed decision about Scientology, the question is not, "Does Scientology work?" The key question is, "Does Scientology work for me?"

MEET THE AUTHOR

Boyd Grant is the youngest of six siblings and was raised in a strict religious family who faithfully attended and practiced the beliefs of the Roman Catholic Church. Throughout his childhood he was forced to regularly attend Sunday school, Sunday Mass, Midnight Mass, Catechism classes, Baptisms, Confession and other miscellaneous church functions.

When Grant turned eighteen, he refused to attend church or practice the beliefs of the Catholic Church. He was partially disowned by his parents and forced to move out of the family home. Grant packed up his belongs and moved across country from the east coast to the west coast, and has not looked back.

Grant has traveled and backpacked through many parts of the country and dabbled in eastern religions and philosophies. He attended a few Scientology meetings in his early twenties, but, as he entered his thirties, he decided he wanted to learn more about the controversies, values, beliefs and myths of Scientology.

Today Grant describes himself as spiritual rather than religious. Boyd encourages everyone to live in the moment and love with an open mind.

In his free time, Grant enjoys surfing, hiking, science fiction and spending time with his fiancée Sue and their rescue dogs Muttley and Thor.

www.ingramcontent.com/pod-product-compliance
Ingram Content Group UK Ltd.
Pitfield, Milton Keynes, MK11 3LW, UK
UKHW022119230426
12048UKWH00010BA/613